A MEMORY OF ELE[PHANTS]

AND OTHER COLLECTIVE NOUNS FOR ANIMALS

WRITTEN BY GUS BERGER • ILLUSTRATIONS BY OLIVER LAKE

A cauldron of hawks in the clouds they roam,

as a memory of elephants find their way home.

A parliament of owls sit and make laws,

as a clutter of cats sharpen their claws.

A bevy of swans quietly talk,

as a gaggle of geese rudely squawk.

A mob of whales gracefully glide,

as a shoal of mackerel
wisely hide.

A shrewdness of bees choose their flowers,

as a rabble of butterflies
flutter for hours.

A slurry of foxes plan the nights' prowl,

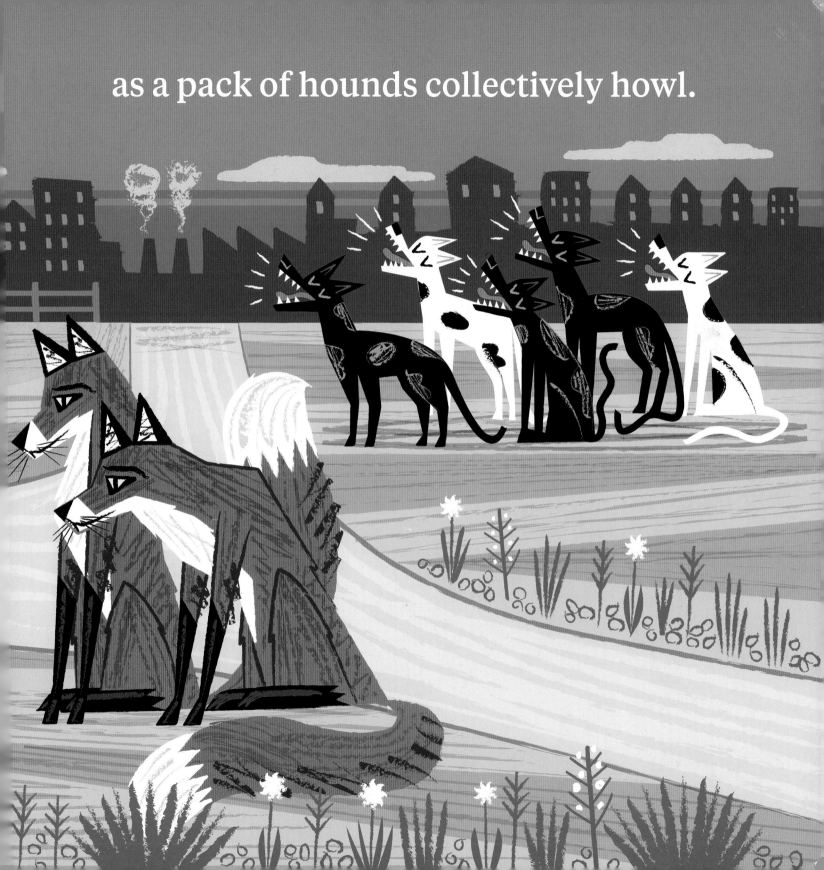

as a pack of hounds collectively howl.

A quiver of cobras standing up straight,

as an ambush of tigers patiently wait.

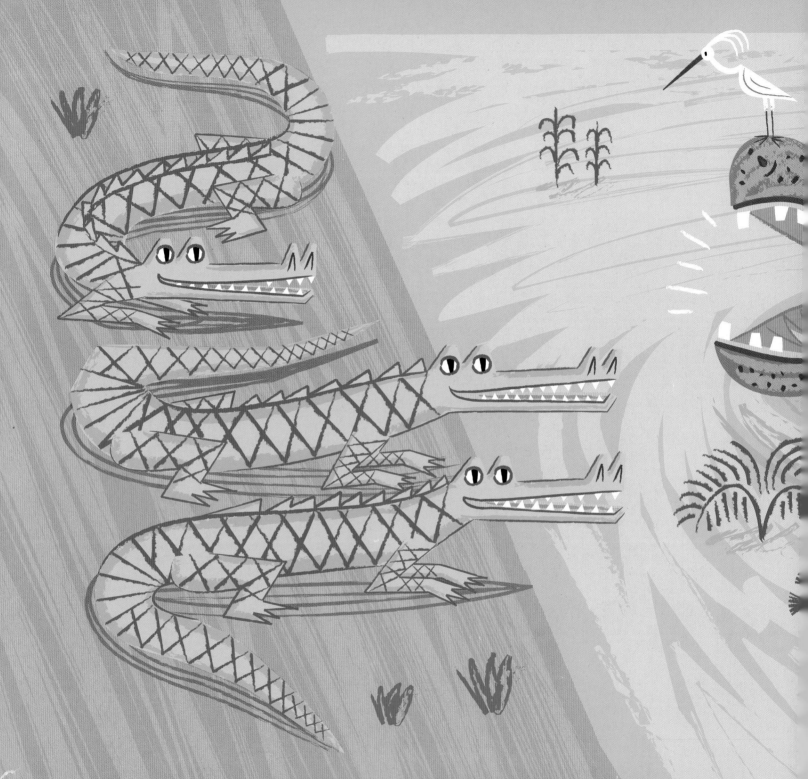

A congregation of crocodiles hangs around,

as a crash of hippos make a frightful sound.

A prickle of hedgehogs
snuffle around,

as a lounge of lizards
sleep on the ground.

A sliver of sharks swim quick as can be,

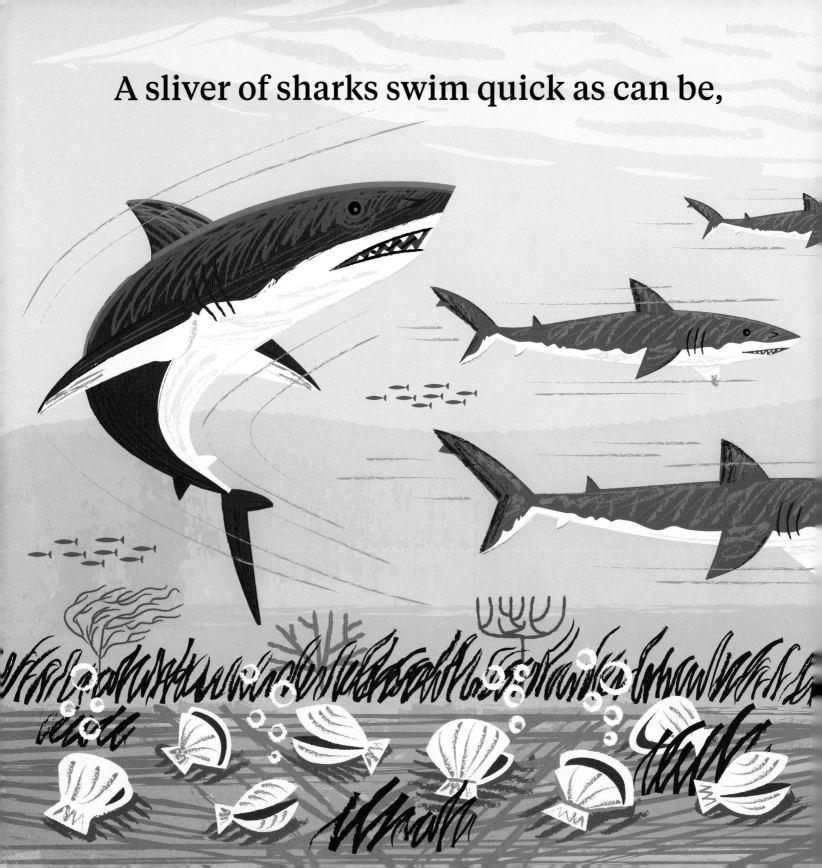

as a bed of clams lie still under sea.

A cackle of hyenas sing out of key,

as a troop of monkeys hide in the tree.

Dedicated to Axel and Moose.

Writing by Gus Berger | gustofilms.com
All artwork © Oliver Lake | iotaillustration.com
Design & Layout by Andy Lewis | studioshapes.com.au
Production supervision by Hannah Howell

Published by Albury books.
Albury Court, Albury, Thame, Oxfordshire, OX9 2LP, Uk
alburybooks.com

Printed in China

ISBN: 978-1-910571-65-1